SUNDOWN

PHOEBE HESKETH

Phoebe Hesketh

Sundowner

London
ENITHARMON PRESS
1992

First published in 1992
by the Enitharmon Press
36 St George's Avenue
London N7 0HD

Distributed in the UK and Ireland
by Password (Books) Ltd.
23 New Mount Street
Manchester M4 4DE

Distributed in the USA
by Dufour Editions Inc.
PO Box 449, Chester Springs
Pennsylvania 19425

© Phoebe Hesketh 1992

ISBN 1 870612 03 5 (paper)
ISBN 1 870612 08 6 (cloth)

The paperback edition is limited to 800 copies
and the cloth edition to 25 copies, signed and
numbered by the author

Set in 10pt Ehrhardt by Bryan Williamson, Darwen
Printed in Great Britain by
Antony Rowe Ltd, Chippenham, Wiltshire

Contents

Being 9
How To Do It 10
Partridge 11
The Third Fox 12
Dower House 13
The Cap 14
July 2nd, 1916 15
Unicorn 16
Olympia 17
Orpheus in the Underground 18
Protean Lover 19
Half a Loaf 20
Love Song 21
Truth Game 22
Perennial Love Song 23
Egotist 24
The Tale of a Frog 25
The Face at the Window 26
Survival 27
Starlings 28
Brain Child 29
The Shaping Spirit 30
Shutting Out the Sun 31
The Dig 32
Lost Childhood 33
No Reply at Christmas 34
Prophet 35
A Jolly Good Fellow 36
The Art of Grief 37
Hurricane David 38
Return 39
Where Dying Begins 40
Hobson's Choice 41
Refugee 42
The Eye 43
Vision 44
My Only Hope is the Sky 45
Edward Thomas 46

The Vale of Seven *47*
Glimpse from the Old Tram Bridge *48*
Master Cotton Spinner *49*
No Certainty *52*
Imprint *53*
All Hallows *54*
Sundowner *55*

ACKNOWLEDGEMENTS

Some of the poems in this collection have previously
been published in the following:
*Acumen, Agenda, Outposts, The Rialto,
The Spectator, Stand, Times Literary Supplement,
Writing Women*

Dedicated to Neil Curry
with thanks for sound advice

Being

Animals do not cling;
They stand
Patient in fields, not waiting.
Unfooled by hope,
Unringed by promises,
Being, not understood
But felt, is all,
Lived breath by breath
In the deep, dark wood of unknowing
Where death, their birthright,
Is not wrapped in words and flowers.

How To Do It

How do the birds do it?
You hear them singing
fit to turn the leaves
and swell the bushes.

See them weaving –
flashing shuttles in-and-out the branches.
But you never see them dying
or even dead.

How do they do it
so tidily there's never a feather
to sweep up from the lawn –
unless the cat's around?

If only we
could emulate the birds and disappear
singing
out of sight and sound.

Partridge

She was round and warm and brown,
homely and soft as a fresh cob loaf.
She nestled you to comfort
from stings of nettles, thistles,
and wasp-thin tongues.
One could feel her
feathering her eggs, folding them
under her breast,
shuffling her wings
till all were safely gathered.

Her warmth of welcome shone
across a field;
you came to her out of the rain;
the wind lay down when she was near.
Sorrow that dropped from you
was dried, and laughter shook
easily as ears of corn.

I never heard her sing;
her song was herself.

The Third Fox

The third fox has never been alive;
His questing nose in redwood points me back
To the first one hunted till his sunset end
In Hangman's Wood, the second,
Mounted for display with amber eyes
Set in glassy stare on passers-by.
Both remembered running, warm
Through this one coiled and still, yet sprung
With innate foxiness.
Unmoving, he moves beyond the snap of hounds
And teeth hidden in unsuspected grass.

Dower House

For twenty-seven years this house has held
Me hostage, bricked me in and bent my will
To do its bidding.
Days after nights I've wept
To wake up to the wheel again, and still
I move between the table and the fire
Wearing a groove that fits me like a shoe;
Have heard the death-watch beetle ticking through
My dreams – a metronome that beats desire
Into still-warm evening ash.
I wake to know my children grown and gone;
The tree tapping the kitchen window bare
To the naked sky. Now sunk in peace, alone
I hate my freedom, dread the silent stair,
The timber-creak at dark, and the heavy door
Without a key that opens to nobody there.

The Cap

After three days dragging
They found him, mouth in the mud, hair
Tangled with weeds and roots of water-lilies;
And here and there about him
Whose careful fly – Dark Snipe and Purple –
Had hovered temptingly,
A trout nosed, curious.

Now was the mayfly season
Which year by year
Had found him standing stiller than a heron
Among the reeds. Patient as a heron while he cast
Again, again above the ruffled water.

He was the archetype of fishermen,
Native to the brown-green silences
Of trout-pool, lake, and river,
Unborn into the world of chattering boxes,
Flickering screens outside his ring of leaves
That greeted his return
Until the day of no return.

Only a gentleman, the searchers said,
Wondering at the order of his going,
Would first take off his cap
And leave it for our guidance on the wall.

July 2nd, 1916

'British Attack on The Somme'

Six o'clock reveille: Scamblers Farm
and a shotgun bolt withdrawn.
Thump on the trestle, the first pig is landed
twisting, screaming; overhead
fantails murmur soft as down
while these, necklaced fine and red
under the accurate knife,
are bubbling, gargling gouts of blood
congealing to rubies
on glistening cobbles and boots.

On my seventh birthday, torn
from a feathered dream, I awake
to nightmare loud and warm
trampling the summer air,
and I'm running, head down, through the gate
shielded by trees to the river.

Unicorn

On the fifth day
the unicorn
must have slipped God's mind
somewhere between horse and goat,
and so was made safe
from man and extinction.
But maybe that
was the primal intention?

Ever seeking a gentle lady
beside whom to lie down,
he travels the world
unguided, invisible.
Archetypal, he faces
the lion beneath the crown.

Beyond this painted emblem
he wanders still,
a shadow seeking the light
in that patient woman who waited
through the dark night of nails
and thorn on the hill.

Olympia

The smooth indifferent moon looked down
On her double, unwrinkled in Alpheus – sacred river
Sounding through Coleridge's broken dream.
For us it girdled Olympia
With memories, rumours
Of discus-throwers through lost centuries.

We'd restored the crumbling pillars with echoes,
Triumphs and disasters; stood
Wordless before the flying feet
Of Hermes immortalized, stone-bound, his face
By magic of Praxiteles
Printed on the future.

Statues, shrines, the empty stadium grassed
From sweat of running feet;
Thundrous Zeus's temple risen from rock –
These recalled as we stood in the moonlit garden
That held its breath with leaves,
Listening
For distant tramping, spears clashing on shields,
Hearing only the wind in the white petals
Of roses caught in the iron balustrade
Till a single nightingale
Aroused the charm to sing the heroes back
From hills of legend and forgotten graves.

Orpheus in the Underground

In the moment of looking back
From the top step
Of the elevator
The white flower of her face
Tilted towards him
Melted into the crowd.
And the tunnel sucked her underground.

The crowd surged upward
Pushing him into
The concrete world,
Mirrors mocked him; voices
Demanded rock for dancing;
Stamping feet stamped on
The hems of grief; breaking
His guitar strings; hands
Unstrung him, flung him
Singing into the Thames.

Protean Lover

I have a lover, but he's made of paper;
I read him back through words unwritten, find
A stranger hidden in the space between
Lines that lead me dancing, leave me blind.

I have a lover, but he's made of glass;
I see straight through him till I only see
My searching eyes reflected and reflecting
Receding images of him in me.

I have a lover, but he's made of water;
Lost to myself I plunge and swim alone
Away from the crumbling shore, compelled by the current
To drink the life I seek until I drown.

Half a Loaf

There are times when half a loaf
Is far more cruel
Than never a bite of bread.
Eternal cold is kinder than the fuel
That kindles hope instead
Of burning down till truth's defiant jewel
Shines where the fire is dead.

Half a loaf in love's name
Feeds the beast
But starves the spirit of man,
A refugee from Agapé's high feast,
He steals what crumbs he can –
Lover into dog, or thief at least,
Or was it a ghost who ran?

Love Song

You to me are a taste
of strychnine that heightens
the day, the world, that lightens
my darker self till shadows
creeping over all retreat
into the body of the tree
that throws them; momently
I am free of myself in re-creation.

Truth Game

He's peeled another skin
off my onion,
and I feel the cold, exposed
naked to truth, as to a knife.
In such undress is no redress – a cut,
because onions cannot bleed,
draws no blood, but peeling
such as his that makes no mark,
allows no healing.

Perennial Love Song

I to you am a shadow
slanting, sometimes, across the page,
in-and-out through chinks unguarded,
present only in secluded corners
when the garden is quiet, the room empty,
echoing around the walls
with words a backward glance recalls.

But you to me are the sun
breaking through protective trivia,
catching me out
in gaps of thought, and when at nights
I try to bury you in books,
a beanstalk sets the green, compulsive ladder
to unimagined heights.

Egotist

While having my say I see him
pawing the ground, reining himself in
to charge the gap in my thought,
to leap in, gallop
over unframed sentences, breaking
my nerve.
I grow small as Alice
facing a tunnel of retreat.

But when he is gone
I am large again
and break through the looking-glass
to my own territory –
a country of listeners
where no one overrides.

The Tale of a Frog

He felt very small inside
so he had to blow himself up
like the frog who a-wooing would go
of a princess, jumped into her lap,

Slept on her pillow, and blew
his praises deep in her ear
while she slept so she never knew
what shape had come near.

She dreamed of a prince, and awoke
to a peacock spreading his tail;
and the sound of a trumpet broke
through her dream, and none could prevail

To melt this enchantment, she vowed
to follow the prince to the close
of each day as the sun through a cloud,
next morning arose

To a peacock's tail brushing the floor,
and the sound of a trumpet played flat;
expecting the prince, she opened the door
to an empty skin stretched on the mat.

The Face at the Window

Each move I make is watched; I dare not breathe
As I rise from my chair to cross the room tiptoe –
The floor may creak; I may be seen, and so
I reach for the table, crouch down underneath.

Those eyes still follow, twist my mind with guilt;
If I could creep away on hands and knees
Maybe I'd shut them out till by degrees
They'd tire of waiting, set me free to melt

Across the carpet, through the door, escape
That black hypnotic stare; I turn my head
Away from the pansy face, the opening red
Of a mouth whose soundless protest is the shape
Of a cave to swallow me; I cannot win,
Must open the window, let the creature in.

Survival

Survival is the Word
Uttered in the egg –
Blackbird swallows silent worm
And turns it into song:
Usurping cuckoo pushes the young
Out of a song-bird's nest.
And where's the foetus needing air
That would not kill its host?

But aphids, labelled double X,
Must have the edge on us –
Virgins all, they reproduce
By parthogenesis.
Aphids eating rosebuds
Are food for ladybirds
Whose scarlet armour is no guard
Against a hungry wren.
Thus united hand-in-glove
With death, life munches on.

Starlings

Starlings have good ears:
they pick up threads of song
from blackbirds, thrushes to deceive us
with variations from chimney-pots.

Starlings fool us
with originality,
cuckooing the lover
with spring rhapsodies,
luring schoolboys out of school.

Starlings are found in libraries,
pecking among bookshops,
nesting a season in museums.
Adept at worming in dictionaries,
darting through leaves
of encyclopaedias, this breed,
crop-full of knowledge,
is practised in the art
of eclectic harvesting
whose corn serves to gloss
their borrowed plumes.

Brain Child

They sit up late
weighing synonyms,
twisting syntax to outwit understanding.
Phrases are scalpelled
in deliberate surgery.

Come dawn, the seed
dug up from the dark bed of unknowing,
is dissected;
labour's brain child analysed,
fragmented, cannot flower.

The Shaping Spirit

As a woman selecting threads
From a swatch of colours,
He selects words
Of many shades, tones, nuances.
Each to be weighed, measured,
Tongue-tested, and applied
According to relevance, shaped
Into stanzas, and what then
But a conglomerate
Of words unfired as a lump of clay
Without the shaping spirit?
Not to be teased into life
By will or desire,
But by giving air and space
To that which, seasoned as wood,
Catches fire.

Shutting Out the Sun

For days he has sat in the dark room
Developing ideas, consulting
References, and drawing
Conclusions unfixed on the film.
Baffled, he tries another take,
Dares not let in the sun –
That would expose another kind of failure.

Running to waste, energy
Spins the weathercock all ways
Sending him about, but not out
Of himself. Which way he goes he returns
To a blind corner
In the dark room.
Which way he stands
He stands in his own light.

The Dig

(In November 1989 a gang of youths dug up the coffin of a young woman, recently buried, and threw it in a nearby field: Coppul, near Chorley, Lancashire)

Here, at night they come
roaring into the silence, baffled
by its constancy, grinding
their brakes into it, dismounting
and walking the slow path where the paving-stones
stand upright, each one named.

Unfulfilled from the last fix,
they remember the spade
propped against the northern wall:
'Here goes, let's dig
into Agnes Mayhew, only twenty-six' –
no moss has blinded her dates.

Six foot deep, sealed up with sorrow she lay.
They tipped her out to rot more openly
on the dump with Easter's altar flowers.
But the brass plate and handles
will carry them over another day.

Lost Childhood

Someone had to do it;
Before birth there was blood
On his forehead,
The umbilical cord fatefully looped
Round his neck.
A whisper in the womb
Had compelled him to attend the feast
With the host
Offering all, speaking in riddles
Of coming and going.

Silent, he listened and kept his place
With right hand dipped in the dish,
Left hand secreting the ace
Of spades up his sleeve.

No Reply at Christmas

I have called you many times;
it's always No Reply.
And the answer from Enquiries
is my own question –
'What town and name?'
when the name's not in the book.

In the dark I go out, walking
through the Christmas wood
where the star that stood over a stable
is under a cloud.

When I ask its position
in the heavens, they laugh deriding
faith in an old story
woven of myth and fairy-tale,
and leave me in the cold
wind blowing away even rags
of comfort.

But I cannot go back –
my footprints are filled with snow,
the track obliterated.
And I cannot go on through the blind
night. I will forget time and the winter,
and wait, not seeing
but hoping.

Prophet

In purple and gold
he towers above them, gathered
to hear his word illuminating
the mystery
absorbed centuries before, imploring
a lead into depths beyond understanding.
But his tongue is a blade
cutting away their ground, upturning
grass they've walked over unquestioning.

With upraised arm
he shows them the keys
and locks them out of the garden.

He lays a pavement before them, crushing
half-opened flowers,
and directs them to shelves of science
and philosophy.
And they come away hearing
the gate closing against them
a second time.

A Jolly Good Fellow

*For he's a jolly good fellow
And so say all of us.*

And who's this jolly good fellow
Who joins in song and dance
And leads us in the chorus, why
It's Jesus!

Come, bring your ukelele
Or maybe a guitar
And play it at the altar;
He likes it better far

Than solemn organ music
And grey repeated chants –
We blow the Master's trumpet
In multi-coloured pants.

Fill up the bath with water
And plunge the baby in
And name it one of us who come
To wash away our sin.

We drink him in Ribena
And eat him in brown bread;
We rock-an'-roll to heaven
And clap our hands instead

Of being still and silent
Before a Mystery:
It is an open secret
Divulged to you and me –
The man is dancing with us
Who died upon a tree.

You can tell the same old story,
Give it another name
But he *is* a jolly good fellow
Just the same.

The Art of Grief

She is practised in grief
and this is an art
requiring suspension
surrender –
loosing the rope
falling
into nobody's arms
becoming nobody
facing the dark
till dark, aware of darkness,
becomes light.

Hurricane David

Hurricane David risen from nowhere
tearing
the world apart, flattening cities,
drowning
men at work and men at prayer,
pulling out forests' hair,
blows order back to chaos,
dust to dust.

Unmanned manic power –
what law does this obey
that crushes without intent
men as men crush flies?
Yet gently turns
with earthworms the earth it splits,
and opens the sky with thunder
as it opens a flower.

Return

I was always away from myself,
a shadow opening
doors without rooms, falling
short of being,
nobody's ghost, seeing
unseen,
a stranger meeting
me face to face in the dark.

Now all the rooms and beds are mine;
I am mistress of the switches.
Darkness rocks me, day
breaks into poetry and music.
No one locks me out of the inner room.

If the house feels empty
I think of those
whose absence has made me someone
I could never have known.

Where Dying Begins

Being born is less difficult;
A struggle, certainly, but the pain
Is another's. There,
Where dying begins
With the first breath,
The pain is one's own.

This circuit of blood will be broken,
And my sheltered heart, like a red flower,
Exposed for insects to eat
And rivals devour.

Must I go
From order and safety to this?
My long swim has brought me
Head on to the sluice-gate.
But I did not ask to be born
Where water and air might kill,
And the axe at the tree root is gilded,
And the birds, like leaves, are silent.

Shall I turn my head upwards,
Stretch out my arms
Before they can give me a name?
Or dare the blind tunnel ahead
Tearing my nails as I grope
Unseeing towards the light?

Hobson's Choice

Now is the time of two choices
Amounting to no choice:
The Waiting Room thinly disguised
As Rest Home with sharp corners cushioned,
Pointlessness blunted and buttered
With phrases that melt away questions
To which are no answers,
Or walking back into the snow
Whose comfort is surer
Than stair-lifts and invalid beds.
No wheelchairs to lengthen the journey,
No need for the needle's deception
Or capsules to quicken the heart –
The choice that is no choice was chosen
Way back at the start.

Refugee

Time moves on; the place remains
Eternally Samaria for me,
A refugee belonging
Less here than anywhere before.
Back there I had seven,
One at a time, of course;
Out here there's no one to own me –
Who'd want a seventh part, anyway?
No one to draw water for
So the well is full,
Full enough for drowning.

The Eye

I fear the giant telescope
Down which God sees the world
When I would be invisible
Even to a closest friend.

The Eye that peers beneath the bush,
Under the blanket, and
Exposes every footprint sunk
Deep in forbidden sand.

I fear the Eye that pierces through
My secret self; I see
What I was blinded by before –
The Eye becoming me.

Vision

Here at the gate where understanding ends
Vision begins, for only silence calls
Louder than any voice, and darkness bends
My stubborn will.
I cannot see the way and yet I pass
Beyond the measured boundaries of mind.
Shine on me as the sun on window-glass
Till I transmit the light I cannot find.

My Only Hope is the Sky

The wide and leafy world has shrunk
To a narrow room:
Bed, chair, commode, the bare
Necessities.

Why this dragnet interim,
The waiting drawn out so
I am is thinned to what I cease to be?

'If I were a bird,' she sighs,
'There'd be the willing flight into a tree,
Descent to sheltering leaves and dark –
The ending hidden from sight.

Now, having no address,
No path or patch of grass,
My only hope is the sky:
I wait the dawn
And watch the corner window fill with light.'

Edward Thomas

Out of the woods he came;
From some green world his other life began
In way-back bondage to a god half man,
Half goat who knew each bird and leaf by name.

Often the stars he wondered at went blind
As he unseeing struggled in the dark,
Brick-walled captive of a searching mind,
Lost to his loved ones, trampling the spark
He lived by in the mud.

Through this quick anger poisoning the blood
There comes a bead of song, a thread of sound
Lifting the choking gloom; he wakes to see
The first primrose, a wood anemone
Pale as a shell from centuries underground.

And the world is light, light as the first day;
Creation holds him singing in its power,
Perceiving truth in beauty hidden away
In a wren's egg, rain, and dust on a nettle flower.

The Vale of Seven

Elegy for an Irish poet

Between the river and the rock he sits
Reflecting on the ashen lake
And how the damson-coloured hills
Dissolve with distance, vanish into dreams.

At the end of thought sometimes
He walks the sandy road beside the water
Observing the ripples, how they slap and sway
The paper reeds and lapse back into silence.

A stranger to himself, he views the past
As through a telescope, to find
Forgotten images with power to kill
A creature in its shell.

This is the Vale of Seven –
Seven crosses and the seven pines
Shielding the roofless church from wind and rain.

On that last day
He knelt before the ruined altar where
Light through a broken window touched his head
As though in benediction. There
He stayed believing
The crumbling stone his true memorial.
A blackbird chimes his thought;
A shot rings out
Scattering the music waiting in the glen.

Now seventeen years have gone
I recreate him out of light and shadow,
Red leaf, blue feather, winter silences
Where snow and wood-smoke weave his words together
For frost to hammer into singing trees.

Glimpse from the Old Tram Bridge

Slugging between banks of rank weed
The river has forgotten its source,
Flowerless, with here and there
A flare of red or blue
Where a plastic bottle tussles with the reeds.

Here once I came to the water running clear –
Not as glass
But rippling pewter caught by changing light.
Long ago on the Old Tram Bridge
As a child I came, and knelt and spied
Between the wooden planks
The river sparkling underneath,
And held my breath in wonder
At the first day of creation –
The day this Age of Progress has carried away
To the darkening sea.

Master Cotton Spinner

Bolton, Lancashire, in the 1950s

The mill's black finger
Thrusting higher through the mist
Than the steeple of St Peter,
Has pointed his childhood to work,
Money, and power at the top,
Shadowed each working hour,
Bricked-in his dreams,
Written his will in a smoke-plume.

Overalled at seventeen,
He trod his father's mill barefoot
On hot, greased boards,
Serving the mules,
Nursing the thread
Into white cocoons, fattened
Upon whirling spindles
In damp heat tasting of oil,
Noise dimming speech to lip-language
As he learned the cool feel
Of cotton ripened by Egyptian sun.

Grading each load, was himself upgraded
To foreman, manager; he remained
Servant of machines, friend of spinners,
Bob, Jim, and Fred in the warm club
Fumed with beer and tobacco,
Refuge and home where differences were levelled
On the same floor.

He played bowls for Hawkshaw's,
Visited them in hospital –
Spinners' cancer fruiting in their vitals
Was reckoned a voluntary, while he
Sat uneasy in his office chair.

Red sky at morning: the spinners' warning;
The rising sun, crimson,
Soundless, sounded a gong
With cheap, bright frocks from Japan,
Gaudy towels from Pakistan
To dazzle in chain-stores.

It was short time for them.
The mill closed one day a week,
And then two.
Idle machines rusted, were scrapped.
His new job was scrapping the older men.
Evenings found him empty, threadbare,
a blind drawn down his face.

Still the colourful bales flowed in
Easy as eastern flowers, cajoling
Buyers to ignore snags in the cloth.

Through silence of spindles and looms,
Queues at the labour exchange,
And rents unpaid, still the flood,
Ominous as the Styx,
Gulped and rose outside the gates.

Seven hours
Round a boardroom table reduced it
To a trickle in the Take Over.
Hawkshaw's brick-built name written
Over a century's endeavour,
Survived on paper – in small print.

New managers were enlisted,
Young men roped against disaster
In competition's tug-of-war.
The last of the old comrades –
Deadwood Jim and Fred, were his for the cutting.

He was a job for the chairman
Who shook his hand, presenting him
With a gold watch and chain.

Unmanned, redundant, unnamed in the crowd,
He watched Hawkshaw's chimney felled like a tree.
But a tree falls whole, stretched proud to its highest leaf;
The doomed chimney collapsed like a toy
Into smoking rubble;
You could hear a sparrow fall
In brick-dust of that choking silence.

He returns daily to tread the mill
In the supermarket risen in its stead,
Fingering tins as he fingered the spindles,
Pulling the years' thread from his ravelled sleeve.

No Certainty

There is no use giving a name
To what is written in the wind,
Signed on the undersides of leaves,
And has no form
Stamped with date of birth,
Present address and nationality,
No identifiable fingerprints.

The archaeologist must accept
The unproven,
And the scientist with test-tube and measure
Acknowledge the coming of night
Without answer.

And what of the theologian
Arguing the unanswerable
That reverberates through centuries
Of spire-building, bell-ringing,
Setting up images, performing
Rituals while the killing goes on?
Only our comings-in and goings-out
Are certain as the seasons.

Imprint

It is a footprint
In sand or snow
With nobody there.

It is a voice.
But when I question, I hear
Only the wind
Fingering dead oak leaves,
Lifting
The stiffened fir tree branches.

It is the form
Of a hare – grasses
Still warm
And rounded from its resting,
But empty as air.

It is nothing and no one
Who can be known,
Only the imprint
Of somebody there.

All Hallows

(for Hilbre)

Walking among the antlered oaks,
Beeches, birches going gold,
Bracken, fox and squirrel-red,
I walk with ghosts.

It's not the sorrow of being old
But simple grief to be the last
Which overlays these coloured joys
With none to share the memoried past
Time only half destroys.

I wait until the ripe sun sets
And watch the trees,
How they count the days with leaves
And no regrets.

Sundowner

In the last light of a late
October day
Let me go like a flake
Of whitening ash as I slowly burn
Down from the sun towards the day's return.